Raised Bed Gardening Planting Guide

The complete guide to growing in raised garden beds

Table of Contents

Introduction iv

Chapter 1: What is Raised Bed Gardening? 1

Chapter 2: Advantages and Disadvantages of Raised Bed Gardening 2

Chapter 3: Site Selection 6

Chapter 4: Raised Bed Design and Materials 8

Chapter 5: Constructing the Raised Bed 13

Chapter 6: Soil and Potting Mixes for Raised Beds 17

Chapter 7: Planting in Raised Beds 19

Chapter 8: Further Tips and Techniques 21

Conclusion 24

Introduction

I want to thank you and congratulate you for downloading the book, *"Raised Bed Gardening Planting Guide"*.

This book contains helpful information about raised bed gardening, what it is, and everything you need to know to get started.

Raised bed gardening has a plethora of benefits, including better quality of plants, a higher yield, and a more attractive garden! As you will see in this book, it's simple to get started.

Throughout the book, we will cover everything you need to know to start raised bed gardening, from how to construct the bed, to choosing the correct soil and location.

This book will explain to you tips and techniques that will help you successfully begin growing in raised garden beds, and will have all the neighbors jealous! Well, what are you waiting for? Read on and begin learning all there is to know about raised bed gardening!

Thanks again for downloading this book, I hope you enjoy it!

Chapter 1: What is Raised Bed Gardening?

Raised bed gardening is a type of gardening in which plants are cultivated and planted on a soil that is essentially higher than the surrounding ground soil. The raised soil can be elevated for a few inches to up to a few feet high. The raised bed soil is enclosed by a frame or edges to prevent it from eroding or spilling out.

Raised bed gardening has been in use in practice for centuries. It was first developed to address the problem of poor drainage in certain types of soils. However, nowadays, raised bed gardening is practiced not only for the benefits it brings regarding drainage, but also for other various reasons. The other advantages, as well as disadvantages of raised bed gardening will be discussed in detail later.

Generally, raised bed gardening was developed for vegetable farming in areas with clay type soils. However, due to its positive effects, it is now also used for other types of plants including fruit producing plants like strawberries, and flowering plants such as dwarf sunflowers.

Starting a raised garden is not rocket science. Even a complete novice with no gardening skill or experience at all can successfully make raised beds and plant crops in it. All you need to have is proper guidance and knowledge of what to do and how to properly do it, which this book will provide!

Chapter 2: Advantages and Disadvantages of Raised Bed Gardening

The use of raised bed gardening has many effects on a garden, whether it be an advantageous one or a disadvantageous one.

Advantages

Generally, the main advantage of raised bed gardening is its improved water drainage. If a hole about a feet and a half deep is filled with water, and an hour later the water is still there, then the soil does not have adequate draining capacity. The soil may be of the clay type or may be too compact and lumpy for the water to pass through effectively. If this is the case, then a gardener may choose between three solutions: install drain tiles, ameliorate the soil through a method called double digging, or just build raised beds. Laying down drain tiles is not only very time consuming, it is also very expensive. Additionally, this method is not always possible for particular towns and suburbs.

On the other hand, double digging is also time consuming and may result in what is called "bath tub effect" wherein great amounts of water collect in a bed area on the soil. So these results only leave one choice for the gardener, the raised bed gardening.

If the soil or any growing medium is raised above normal level, then the tendency is for it to drain quicker than normal. In addition, raised soil also heats up faster, intensifying the evaporation rate, thereby preventing the accumulation of excess moisture. Not only that, the extra heat generated from raised beds is also valuable in the germination of planted seeds. Heat is one of the factors that dictate whether a seed will grow into a seedling or just become inactivated.

Aside from this, raised beds can also be filled with high quality growing media or soil mixes. This can help as well regarding the soil's drainage capacity. It also gives a more defined and complete nutrient level, resulting to faster growth rate, less maintenance, easier harvest, and higher yield of produce.

Another advantage of raised bed gardening is its practicality in terms of space accessible to the gardener. Raised bed gardens can aid in maximizing the usage of space available for planting. This is obviously a benefit for those people who only have a small plot wherein they could plant. It can also be a solution for those people who have a plot to cultivate, but are in a sloping or inclined area. This is because building a raised bed allows one to control the flatness or the degree of slope of the raised bed.

Raised bed gardening also produces higher yield in proportion to the area planted. Raised bed gardening allows for a denser planting technique, which results to larger production per square foot of soil. This denser planting system is also effective in the clearing, reduction, and prevention of further germination of weeds.

People also utilize raised bed gardening for their hassle-free maintenance. In raised bed gardening, the soil can be maintained easily primarily because of its confined growing media. The definite amount of soil in the bed is also paramount in the lessening of maintenance due to the compaction of soils.

Lastly, raised beds can be a prized addition to one's own garden or backyard. With just a few proper arrangements and designs, the formality and order of the raised beds can certainly be an eye candy to everybody who passes by.

Disadvantages

Although raised bed gardening presents many beneficial features, like all things, raised bed gardening also comes with some disadvantages that you need to be aware of.

The primary negative side effect of raised bed gardening is also one of its positive effects. With the elevated beds being heated up more rapidly than those in the ground surface level, drought may be prevalent during the extreme heat of summer. Due to this, additional watering and observation may be necessary to prevent drying out of plants.

Another disadvantage of raised bed gardening is its additional cost. Unlike in conventional gardening wherein a person just plants directly to the soil, raised bed gardening requires materials to build frames or edges and maybe some soil materials, additives, or growing mixes. These products certainly require money. The cost may be lessened by buying cheap framing materials, but the aesthetic value of the bed may suffer.

One more disadvantage of raised bed gardening is its susceptibility to soil-borne disease pressure. This is due to the limited crop rotation. The limited rotation of crops in raised beds may also cause nematode problems aside from soil-borne diseases.

With the increased plant density in raised beds, pest prevalence may present itself to be a problem. This is especially true in the case of foliar diseases. Increased density of planting makes it easy for diseases to develop and spread from one plant to another.

Lastly, raised beds are not suitable for certain types of plants. An example of a plant that is not suitable for planting in raised beds is the watermelon. Watermelon is not fit to be planted in raised beds because it is a sprawling and expansive plant.

Chapter 3: Site Selection

While it is true that raised bed gardening allows a person to practically plant anywhere they desire, a good site in building raised beds is very crucial for the optimum growth of plants. This is why the site for placing raised beds should be carefully pondered upon.

The first thing to consider when constructing a raised bed is the sunlight. A plant generally requires at least six to eight hours of full sun a day. A gardener should expect leggy plants when the raised bed is built on a place which receives very little sunlight. Production and stunted growth may also be expected if this is the case.

However if the only option there is, is a place which receives less than six hours of sunlight a day, a gardener should opt to build the raised garden in an area which receives morning sunlight rather than afternoon sunlight. This is because morning sunlight is generally better compared to afternoon sunlight in terms of vitamin release, Ultraviolet ray emission, and radiation level.

Also, one should avoid building raised beds near trees or large shrubs. The roots of these will probably grow big and creep up the soil of the raised bed. The leaves of the trees and shrubs may also block the sunlight being received by the plants in the raised bed. Another thing is that trees and large shrubs are prone to ant infestation. Ants may build their nest near the trees and damage the plants in the nearby raised bed.

Before building a raised bed, it is important to know what kinds of plant will be cultivated. This is very important if the only site available is very shady. If this is the case, then plants that tolerate little sunlight should be planted. Examples of these are the cool season vegetables like cabbage, lettuce, and broccoli. Some plants, like ornamental flowering plants, also grow with little sunlight or in partial shade.

If the region is very windy, it is best to build the raised bed in an area where it will be protected from strong gusts of wind. Recommended areas include near buildings, fences, or other sturdy structures.

Raised beds should also not be located in places with poor air circulation or those in frost pockets. This is because fungal diseases thrive best in cold areas with reduced air flow. Fungi are quite parasitic, and may impair the proper growth of plants.

For practical reasons and ease of maintenance, raised beds should be built near a water source. Building the raised bed near the water source will greatly reduce the effort of the gardener when watering the plants.

Lastly, if you plan to build more than one raised bed, you should carefully consider the spacing between the beds. The spacing should be wide enough for a wheelbarrow to move through, but not too wide that extra space will be wasted.

Chapter 4: Raised Bed Design and Materials

As for design, a raised bed can be formal or informal. A formal raised bed is suitable for growing ornamental plants and flowers. This kind of raised bed is usually located at the front of the house or any area with high visibility. The border of a formal raised bed is usually made from high quality and expensive materials to look more attractive. Its shape is almost always rectangular. An informal raised bed, on the other hand, is often irregular in shape. The materials used for its frame can be anything from scrap wood to unpolished stones. This raised bed is normally placed in the private parts of the house, usually the backyard, for it may be an eye sore to the general landscape of the front garden. Vegetables are usually cultivated in an informal raised bed.

An effective raised bed used in gardening is not always very deep. Usually, eight to twelve inches of elevation is adequate enough for plants to grow amply. However, depending on the plant, this may vary. For example, most species of vegetable plants needs 12 to 18 inches of elevation for they need drier soil. Drainage is also an important factor in considering the height of the bed. Drainage problems can sufficiently be addressed by raising the bed higher the more inadequate the drainage is.

The raised bed is ideally around four feet in width. This will allow you to reach the center of the bed from either side without stepping onto the bed, keeping the soil compaction at minimum.

At its simplest, a raised bed can be just soil piled and mounded until it significantly reaches a height above the surface ground. However, a raised bed which lacks any kind of frame tends to require more watering because water can escape the raised bed. In addition, without frames, the soil or the growing media will likely erode during repeated watering or heavy rainfall.

Because the frame is the one that holds the soil in the bed in place, the material to be used should be durable, stable, and optionally, attractive. The material should be durable to avoid breakage. It should also be stable to prevent erosion or cracking of the soil being held in place. It should also be attractive enough to achieve a look that will blend in with the surrounding landscape.

When choosing the framing material to be used in raised beds, there are three options: the use of metal, wood, or masonry.

Metal

Metal framing can be just scraps lying around the house or it can be bought from a construction supply store. If scraps are used, the gardener will be spared from the costs of buying new framing materials. However, scrap metals are generally not visually attractive unless extra designs are incorporated or the plants to be cultivated will grow to cover the frame. It really depends on how picky you are with the physical appearance whether you go this route.

Scrap metals are also very prone to rust. Store bought metal edgings, on the other hand can be quite expensive. However, it is best suited for framing curved beds for metal strips can bend easily to contour the outline of the bed. It is also much more attractive than scrap metals.

Wood

Wood is the second option as material for the frame of the raised bed. When used, it gives the bed a very rural or country appearance.

There are several types of wood that can be used to frame a raised bed. These are the natural wood, pressure-treated wood, the landscape lumber, and the synthetic lumber.

Natural woods are woods that are not treated with any kind of chemical or did not undergo any process. This kind of wood is very suitable for organic gardeners as they do not emit any substance that can affect the organic status of the plant. However, natural woods are very prone to deterioration, especially in those regions that experience frequent rainfall. Moisture greatly accelerates the decline of natural woods. Aside from water, wood-boring insects may also present to be a problem. Certain types of insects may chew on the wood, causing it to deteriorate. Due to this, wood that has natural resistance to insects should be used. Example of this is the heartwood of red cedar. For protection, no wood preservative may work with natural woods. On site application of wood preservatives will only protect the wood superficially. Deterioration is expected within one to two years.

The second type of wood is the pressure treated wood. This type of wood is treated by means of a chemical preservative. The chemical preservative is forced to penetrate the wood under pressure. However, there are some issues regarding the utilization of pressure treated wood in gardening, especially when planting vegetables or fruits. Chemicals may leach out of the wood when used as a frame. The chemicals may then be absorbed by the plant and subsequently eaten by humans. However, on the bright side, studies reveal that the chemicals emitted from treated woods are within the safe level of consumption. But to be sure, the interior side of the wood may be lined with a protective barrier like polyethylene, roofing felt, oil-based sealer, or heavy plastic bag.

The third type of wood is called landscape lumber. This is the center of a log whose top and bottom surfaces are machined flat so they can be stacked. The sides of the lumber remain round. This lumber is also dipped in preservative, but penetration is just in the surface so it will not last as long as pressure treated wood, but may last longer than natural wood.

The last type is the synthetic lumber. Synthetic lumbers are manufactured wood that are made from recycled plastic materials and waste wood fibers. Due to this makeup, they have the property to resist insect attack and deterioration even with constant contact to the ground. They are also very garden-friendly for they do not contain any toxic preservatives. Also as an upside, synthetic lumbers do not crack and splinter. But as downside, this type of lumber is very expensive compared to the other type of wood framing materials. They are also not very good when exposed to intense ultraviolet radiation. Also as a minor problem, synthetic lumbers are prone to mildew when they remain in the shade.

Masonry

In constructing raised beds, stones, bricks, or pre-cast concrete can also be used. Depending on what kind of masonry is used, the raised bed can look very appealing to the eye with its natural stone finish.

The main advantage of this material is that it is very durable. Its strength is further intensified when mortar is used during construction. Some products may not even need the use a mortar when being keyed together. This material requires little skill in assembling, but can be very dangerous when using heavy stones or bricks, so be careful. A level surface for the walls should be used when not using a mortar. The walls of the frame should also be only about two courses tall for optimum strength.

For the cost, masonry materials can be both inexpensive and expensive. Concrete building blocks like hollow blocks are generally inexpensive. However, those that do not require mortar and those that can give a natural stone finish can be quite costly.

Chapter 5: Constructing the Raised Bed

Laying Out the Perimeter

Before putting the frame in place, an outline or guide regarding the perimeter of the bed must be laid out first.

If the desired raised bed is square or rectangular in shape, then the edges must have straight lines. Stakes must be placed on each corner of the perimeter. Then the edges are marked by tying the strings to the stakes to outline the whole perimeter. The straight edged raised beds are suitable for vegetable growing for these often require planting in rows.

On the other hand, raised beds can be irregular or curved in shape. This kind of raised bed is commonly used in flowering plants or for aesthetic purpose. When outlining a curved bed, a rope or a garden hose works perfectly well. The rope must be laid down first tracing the perimeter of the bed so the gardener may preview it in the landscape. It is also best if the curves are set to be long and flowing rather than tight and numerous. This is for ease of maintenance particularly mowing the ground lawn.

When outlining, it is also essential to mind the surface level of the bed. In inclined areas, the surface of the slopes must be level or flat.

Removal of Existing Vegetation

Before the frame edges can be installed, existing vegetation around where the raised bed is to be constructed should first be removed.

For the removal of unwanted plants, hand pulling is the most effective way, especially if the area is just small. For a bigger area, a plastic bag is used to cover the plants. The plastic should be anchored by weights such as rocks to avoid being blown off. The heat that will be generated under the plastic will kill grasses and small plants in the area in a span of one to two months. If on a rush, herbicides can be used. The use of herbicides should only be a last resort for it may pose potential toxicity to the non-target plants and also to humans. If herbicides will be used, it is best to assure that it is compatible with any crop, especially food crops that will be cultivated.

For heavy brushes and woody plants, chainsaws or heavy duty mowers can be used for clearing. For trees on the other hand, it is best to call first local authorities to see if any permit is necessary.

Installation of the Frame

If the framing material to be used is metal, the ground must first be watered so the soil will soften. If the soil in the ground is still hard and dry, excavation of the soil to accommodate the edging may be necessary.

Metal frames are usually metal strips with varying lengths. They can be four inches up to six inches wide. Each strip has notches that overlap with other metal strips. This notch is where the stakes are inserted for the connection of the metals. The metal is hammered down into the soil using a rubber mallet. It is best if the metal strips are partially sunk down the soil to hold them in place. After all are in place, the metals are hammered down more until it reaches the desired depth.

For bricks or cinder blocks, a concrete footer measuring a foot high and eighteen inches wide is first poured. This will serve as the wall's base. After the concrete footer is poured, a reinforcing rod is added to the center to increase stability. After three to four days, the footer will be cured. A mortar is then applied down the slab. The first brick is subsequently placed gently. Additional mortar is added to the bricks side, and then the next brick is installed. This process is continued until the frame is completed.

If stones are to be used for raised bed frame, it is recommended to employ professionals for assistance because working with heavy stones can be quite hazardous. The stones are first lined along the perimeter of the frame. The frame should be wider at the base than at the top for stability. Making the wall lean slightly inward may also help increase firmness. If the stone wall is to be made more than one layer thick, then wooden pegs should be used to keep the stones in place. Before setting the new layer, mortar is applied first at the top of the bottom layer. The laying of the stones is continued until it reaches the desired height.

For board woods, the end of each plank is drilled first. Then metal braces and screws are used in the corners for fastening. Nails are generally not recommended for they may split the wood in two pieces. Pre drilling holes can be a good tactic. The completed wood edges are then hammered down the ground until it reaches the desired depth.

Lastly for lumber or timber, the perimeter is first leveled off or set at the wanted slope. The lumber is laid at the perimeter and then secured by driving rebar through a drilled hole in the lumber into the ground. Additional layers of lumber is stacked on top of the bottom layers and then secured also by rebar or spikes. The spikes should extend deeply into the lumber at the bottom layer to ensure stability.

Pre-Made Garden Beds

Another alternative is purchasing a professionally made raised bed. These can be a huge time saver, and can often be quite inexpensive. Check places like craigslist or eBay for these.

Chapter 6: Soil and Potting Mixes for Raised Beds

In general, soil found in one's garden or backyard can be used to fill the raised bed, provided that it meets the plant's requirement regarding drainage and nutrients.

However, if the area lacks appropriate soil, different growing media can be used. There are many premixed soil mixes available in gardening centers. This type of growing media is usually very good for the plant because it is ensured of good drainage, consistency, and nutrition. However, store bought premixed growing media can be quite costly, especially when filling large beds. This is why adequate knowledge regarding mixing raw materials to make growing media is necessary.

The most recommended mix for raised beds is as follows: mixing of six parts pine bark mulch, one part sand, 10 lb. limestone per cu. yd., and 14 lb. slow release fertilizer high in nitrogen. It is recommended to use a fertilizer which contains three times more nitrogen than oxygen and phosphorus.

Another variation in mixing growing media is mixing of four parts pine bark, one part peat, 10 lb. limestone per cu. yd., and 14 lb. of fertilizer with micronutrients per cu. yd.

The mixes stated are just the standard mixes. It may be used for trials, or it may be used permanently. Basically, the type of growing media a gardener should use is the one suitable for your own planting style and the specific plant's requirements. The standard mixes may be tweaked, changed, or even discarded if it does not do well for a gardener.

Chapter 7: Planting in Raised Beds

Plants can be grown by directly planting the seeds in the raised bed or germinating them first at seedling trays.

Germinating the seeds first at seedling trays allows the gardener to grow many seeds at once and then choose the superior seedlings among the batch. This technique also usually has a higher germination rate compared to direct planting because each seed can be taken care of individually.

However, if no seedling tray is available or you find it time consuming to transplant seedlings from the tray to the seedling bed, direct planting can also be done. Because the raised bed essentially has improved soil and the need to walk through between plants is eliminated, more seeds can be planted in an area. Seeds can just be scattered on the bed. Just to make sure, the seeds should be spread very well and evenly across the bed to allow proper spacing for growing. Seeds can also be sown in shallow furrows. Planting in furrows make a more appealing sight and more organized planting, growing, and harvesting.

Fundamentally, most plants can be grown in raised beds. However, different species have various requirements for their optimum growth. Before planting, a gardener should check the pack of the seed to know the requirement of the plant regarding spacing, planting time, orientation, moisture threshold, and harvest time.

Planting in raised beds just improves the condition for the growth of the plant. But in the end, it is still up to the gardener's passion and skill whether the plant will grow or die. Remember to check your plants regularly to ensure they have enough water and sunlight, and are growing healthily.

Chapter 8: Further Tips and Techniques

1.	Mulching is an important part of planting in raised beds. Mulching keeps the roots of the plant cool during hot days, reduces evaporation of water, controls erosion by slowing and softening the impact of water and rain to the soil, and inhibits the growth of weeds. Additionally, mulch can improve the appearance of the raised bed.

After plants grow considerably in the raised bed, a two to three inch layer of mulch can be applied. The mulch should taper to the base of the plants. The amount of mulch needed for a raised bed is computed by multiplying the length of the bed by its width and the depth of the mulch that the gardener wants. The product is then divided by twelve, and then again by 27. The resulting number will be the amount of mulch in cubic yards.

Pine and bark needles are the most commonly used materials for mulching. If not available, shredded newspapers or strips of plastic can also be used. However, these materials should only be used in private areas as they are not attractive to see.

2.	Especially for older people, elevated beds can be very useful. Elevated beds are made by making a planted box with a wooden floor. The flooring should have enough number and proper size of holes for proper drainage. Then legs are added to the bed for wheelchair access or for those people who are not able to bend over.

3.   For protection against birds and insects, the addition of row covers may be necessary. Metal wire hoops or plastic tubing can be utilized as frame or support for the net which will later be installed.

4.   Cultivation of plants according to their time of maturity and length of productivity will greatly increase the efficiency of the raised bed. Planting all short season crops in one area allows the gardener to harvest all the crops simultaneously and immediately replace the harvested crops with other crops that are suitable for whatever the coming season is.

5.   Inter-planting crops is an effective way to make use of all the empty spaces in the raised bed. Inter-planting crops means planting a specific plant A in between rows of specific plant B. In this method, specific plant B can be harvested by the time specific plant A is growing. This reduces the conflicts between different species of plants planted near each other.

6.   Growing plants with the same water requirement in the same area is very convenient in terms of watering. When different species of plants with different water requirements are grouped together, excess or deficit in hydration may prevail in some plants.

7.   Trellises can be added to a raised bed to allow growing of some sprawling plants. These trellises should be oriented to the north end of the bed to avoid blocking of sunlight to neighboring plants.

8.   Diseases in plants, especially vegetables can be minimized by watering early in the morning and keeping water off the foliage.

9.   Fertilizers may be used occasionally, but over fertilizing should be avoided as it can cause excessive plant

growth. Excessive plant growth will result to a very unstable and uneven plant.

Conclusion

Thank you again for downloading this book!

I hope this book was able to help you learn more about raised bed gardening.

The next step is to put this information to use, and begin working on your raised garden beds! Remember to carefully select building materials that will suit your garden, and budget!

Carefully pick what plants you will grow, and where to grow them. Ensure they will get enough sunlight, and will be free from insects.

Finally, be consistent with your gardening, and constantly check the health of your plants to ensure optimum growth!

Also, don't forget to claim your FREE bonus e-book on how to grow tomatoes!

Download your copy at the link below:

http://bit.ly/1ODGQbJ

Lastly, if you enjoyed this book, please take the time to share your thoughts and post a review on Amazon. It'd be greatly appreciated!

Thank you and good luck!

www.ingramcontent.com/pod-product-compliance
Lightning Source LLC
LaVergne TN
LVHW021748060526
838200LV00052B/3541